ENTRIES

Also by Mimi Khalvati

In White Ink
Mirrorwork

Mimi Khalvati

ENTRIES ON LIGHT

CARCANET

First published in 1997 by
Carcanet Press Limited
4th Floor, Conavon Court
12-16 Blackfriars Street
Manchester M3 5BQ

Copyright © Mimi Khalvati 1997

The right of Mimi Khalvati to be identified
as the author of this work has been asserted
by her in accordance with the Copyright,
Designs and Patents Act of 1988
All rights reserved

A CIP catalogue record for this book
is available from the British Library
ISBN 1 85754 329 7

The publisher acknowledges financial assistance
from the Arts Council of England

Set in 10pt Garamond Simoncini by Bryan Williamson, Frome
Printed and bound in England by SRP Ltd, Exeter

For my mother

Acknowledgements

Acknowledgements are made to the editors of the following publications in which some of these poems have appeared:

Acumen, Oasis, PN Review, Poetry London Newsletter, Poetry Review, Sheffield Thursday, The North, The Swansea Review, Transitions, Wasafiri.

Contents

With the exception of the opening and closing passages, each entry is limited to a single page.

Knocking on the door
    you open, after every
absence – yours or mine –
    as our grounds and elevations
realign themselves, you
    on the step below me, one
or both of the kids above
    I'm struck again as you
face me, turn your back, stricken
    by how small you are.

Bird mother, busy woodland
    creature mother
beginning-small and ending-small
    I don't believe that it's only
a kernel blown to husk
    the great revolve and vanishing-
point of our figure of eight
    as you cross the kitchen, lower
the gas and we, entering
    let the small shock pass

that is the shock: for
    watching your anxious steps
vanishing deep down corridors
    to return with gifts, it's more
with a sense of vastness, height
    that I see you shrink;
of radiance, like your candle
    lit in the daytime, that I notice
how pale your hair and skin seem
    beside ours.

Dwindling, as hollows
    deepen, brighten and what is
nearest catches light
    in the circle you inhabit and I
inherit, knowing my reach is smaller
    much too small to lift
and shawl you in my arms, fading
    you intensify, like candlelight
on scalloped lace, in the pink
    the very fabric of our lives.

*

Sunday. I woke
   from a raucous night of
seagulls, shafts of sun
   in old bazaars where motes spun

on an abacus for angels.
   Do you long
to go back to that childhood
   the angels asked

in a grown-up body?
   the everlasting blue enquired
as I woke
   to skies washed clean of dust

and churchbells.
   From the acorn of the blind
such seas came
   such tall grave oaks!

Acorn-greys
   of the sea, its pennant rocks
where cormorant wings
   are omens . . . *Do you long*

to go back to that childhood
   the waters asked
in a grown-up body?
   the everlasting shore enquired

with a cockerel
   to wake me in the morning
a dog to guard us
   through the night, one window

pink with sunset, one blue
   with dusk? I could go on and on.
But I am moving into the morning.
   I am making do with light.

Today's grey light
  is of
light withheld but
  softly
shyly like a sheltered
  girl's.

It's a
  light in gentle
motion
  like a young girl
sitting
  splaying her skirts

her listening smiles
  around her.
When
  barefoot
she disappears
  momentarily to another

sky
  gleams like glassware
we can hear not see
  we
contract but air
  expands

into a memory
  she has thrown
behind her.
  And in the memory is
light
  and lightness.

Scales are evenly
    weighed, inside
outside. Light is
    evenly poised
– blur to the gold
    glare to the blue –
it's twilight.
    In two minds.

Who can read by
    a lamp, focus
land's outline?
    But blue soon
sinks and gold
    rises. Who
can stay the balance
    if light can't?

Streetlamps
    threw battlements of
shadow on a lawn, somewhere
    a travelling

clock ticked; rockplants
    hung faceted
with lurid
    orange raindrops

dustbin lids
    gleamed
under gutter-pipes
    and eaves.

But given
    the minerality of
shorelife, rain's afterlife
    it seemed

with a moon in the sky
    tide going out – and
wave coming in on wave –
    a miracle

that the one should draw
    the other, as though
gravity were more to do
    with weightlessness than weight.

The heavier, fuller, breast
    and body grow, the higher
flies the thought, the more
    rarefied its air.

It is the law of action:
    the stronger a gesture, the lighter
its recovery. On a black sea
    how far the spirit sails!

Through me light drives
   on seawall, fencepost, brittle
spears of lavender. A light
   at its most inexplicable.
In reversals, shadows, replications
   of a ceiling light, table lamp

amber stars that now signal
   now don't, across water.
A world turned back-to-front
   where natural arbiters
of light, sea and sky
   are silenced. Light on

passers-by, dimpled on the gloss
   of windowsills and who knows
if foliage shadowed on stone
   is from creeper or curtain?
Even our image in glass, like knowledge
   forgotten, startles us. How bright

the lamp is in the garden!
   Between this world and the next
runs a white rail to impede
   our fall, illuminate
our light-world's edge, the selvage
   of our small front gardens.

In the amber
    are the leather globe, quillpen;
bald velvet, Red
    Admirals, in the amber are their leaded

lines, candle weeping at the window
    a husband's shirt hung up
to dry, a crib
    and a child's turned head.

In the amber is the smell of
    fox, rosin, stale
tobacco, in the amber is the hallowed glow
    of something old, and male.

The air is the hide
    of a white bull, the light
as tame. But if a storm brews
    this afternoon
when bladderwrack will be
    black at his hooves
and the first white waves
    lather him up into seafoam

she will mount him, rein him
    in with the right horn
and as shorelights fade
    riding oblivion back into time
where the light of the rosehip
    founders, see
tameness
    reveal its astonishing face.

I'm silenced in.
  Bowled over. No
globe so round, star
  as silver, though I've
seen a thousand
  suns, ever rose
like this, a sun
  of grapefruit silver.

Ghostliest of
  beginnings:
a nocturne in the morning
  a Shangri-La
in the upper pane, turn off
  the light, let
acid glow
  from every angle.

One empty room
  can't see it, walk down
the street you'll never
  catch it, even the skylights'
gold denies
  a white eye holed
into the mind of heaven.
  For a moment I was

threatened. Depend on it
  the sun, the moon
depend on him
  who loves you, even
the moon can rise in the morning
  Shangri-La come to town
the beautiful
  be terror.

I hear myself in the loudness
  of overbearing waves, you
in the soft retreat, if-and-but
  of withdrawing sighs, the tug
that gets me nowhere.
  It'll never end. Sound
of the sea – still Sappho's sea –
  the yes-and-no of lovers.

Inland, I dreamt of hearing
  waves again but here
sea in my ears, watching reds
  of life-jackets, blues
of a hull and sails, recapture
  in the yes-and-no of my own blood
only the to-and-fro of our endless
  drift – my bed a beach, you said.

Everything I ever said about you
  was true; but trueness
in that tone and at that pitch
  never helps. How could we help
having loved elsewhere too much
  and I don't mean other lovers
but homelands, other cultures
  pulling oceans in their wake?

Speak to me as shadows do
   where light comes through
perforations of snow-white lace

attenuating on a surface
   eyelets into ovals
softening prisms into flakes.

Speak to me as echoes do
   attenuating, softening
the thing first harshly said.

This book is a seagull whose wings
   you hold, reading journeys between
its feathers. It flutters, dazzles.
   Sings cleanly in shade. Sharpens
your ears to journeys life's taken
   that scraping of a mudguard, tinkling
of stays. Its spine has halved the sun.
   Sun fired it with a nimbus.
A wheelchair passes, crunching on shingle.
   This book, set off by wind, makes you
long for the world, to take lungfuls
   of pleasure, save scraps on quick raids.
So that sated, you turn, blot out the world
   enter another, settle for words.

I'm opening
   the door of shadow
on a page. In the doorway
   stands a poem

like a girl in a dress.
   I see through her
to her feelings –
   absent on the page, absent

as a house might be
   through an overgrowth
of ivy – his
   heart, his despair.

She wants him
   not to talk of
leaves, nor to stand
   in sunlight.

To close the door
   on strangers, lie on her
as a yellow page
   might close on grey.

Not a sheet
   between them, not even
the gap where a thumb
   disengaged.

One upper pane by a windchime
    her moon shines through;
plants, tall or hanging, are
    reminiscent of tunnelled trees
while a fern at eye-level
    confirms some forest floor.

Out there a dog barks rapturously;
    nearer home her cat, whose kittens
died in the litter, scrabbles earth
    with nonchalance, jet streaming
down her coat. How does one invade
    people's spaces with such ease

or people's bodies for that matter
    and is this bad or good?
As natural a brutality as is
    natural to commingle
breath, moisture, soil and seed
    in the underbrush of woods?

I've never been in a hurry
    to find you out, letting
you pledge yourself
    to the oracular. Once

I might have been
    a cabin in the woods
a patch of grass where you studied
    Latin verbs with a friend

who studied you
    so you began to have a sense
of friendship and with it
    loneliness.

I came to you
    through a woman once
who missed me, with you around
    and wanted the three of us

to make space and time
    for a taste
of my vernacular. Now
    with my name on your lips

and hers wiped off, she thinks:
    I thought you weren't
interested – you said you weren't –
    in *happiness*.

It's all very well
    for me you think and I
for trees and sky and wind;
    blind to the grief
beyond our walls, who can tell
    what shadow falls, or leaf?

Show, show me.
    But you see
only through the lens
    of your own eye. Light
strikes your bed
    differently
towerblocks I like to see in a
    cityscape at night
loose screams you hear
    differently – such
fortresses we are.
    Show, show me.

Let the blind lead the blind?
    But we're not. We see
a burnstripe on an arm
    mole, hair
utopias emitting light
    that strikes differently
or fails to light.
    Not isolation
but the singularity of thought
    – thought that freeze-frames
feelings
    we might have had in common –

is the fortress that I plead from
    and am heard
bell-like
    in the service of your own life
lovingly and with empathy
    but when it comes to mine
how should I
    have the heart to tell you, *show* you
that it's not the scream
    in my throat, nor the thought
in my head, nor the light of beliefs
    I steer by?

: that sky and light and colour
   cloud, clearings

should raise me, strip me down
   to the bare bones

of vocabulary – rise fall sea sky
   a tree and not a sycamore

flower and not a bluebell
   till the agony of daily life

falls away, like ground from a tilting
   plane, drops far below me.

I love all things in miniature
    – the blue tree whose sprigs
are like the lilac's in miniature –
    and small things too since they
recollect a child's eye view
    of a small world inside a large
in which small things might represent
    the large – acorn cup a cup, sprig
a tree – and because miniatures are
    fully-formed and in completion
futureless, as if childhood itself
    were arrested, made redeemable.

Lying belly down on grass, level
    with a sparrow's eye as it cocks
its head, engages without seeing us
    I remember how our first lessons
were tailored to a scale in which
    the child loomed large, creatures
small and therefore it was incumbent
    on our stature to feel tenderness.
I felt it for a moment and have lost it
    now that the mind has taken flight
left a birdless stretch of grass
    so much larger than itself.

In that childhood time
of peering out
from a hut of leaves
at the ebb and flow –

though little did
sun perhaps on a glint
of straw, wind
ballooning a shirt or branch –

each gust and pause, drift
of skin between
warm and cold, was a source
of mindless patience.

How a world could be
changed from moment
to moment, broken
by sudden entrances

a bumblebee, helicopter;
resumed and our
solitude, brushing wings
with its passing by

be, for the contact
safer: this
was the ebb and flow
we watched for

as though each shift of
grass, flight of paper
float of shadow across a path
weren't just earth's

response to a moving heaven
but the heart's reply
shaping life
and we its recording angel.

Light's taking a bath tonight
    in the sea's enamelled
blue-rimmed bath, lying along
    its length. Hair submerged
thighs and belly in mile-long
    strips showing through white
between limbs and fingers
    bluer depths.

Light's closing her eyes
    not once but twice – once
face up, once facing down
    from her ceiling mirror.
In rising steam, the longest
    bath earth's ever seen, closing
her lids on sea and sky till only
    mist and vapour stir.

Dawn paves its own way
    if what we mean by dawn
is sunrise. The sky's already
    light by the time the sun
comes up, rising on its own
    prediction of the day.
This is how art is made.
    And memory. And love.

First, the halo overhead.
    Next, the body. Last
the roots like the final
    rays of the sun spiralling
as earth pulls free of them
    and they of earth. Then
illumination's width and frame.
    This is how love is made

rising into a desire
    for love, however grey
the outlook, late the hour
    hard for faith and fear
to pave the way. Love
    full-face. Preordained
as sunrise, chasing after
    the ghost of its own grace.

With finest needles
    finest beads
lawn and dew are making
    a tapestry of water . . .

When sky paints itself
    with daubs and puffs of
cloud-sponge, wrinkles
    the silk surface of the sea, trails
fingers of light on a misted
    ground to illuminate
its manuscript
    what should I do
but put down my pen, marvel
    at its changes before the marvellous
puts away its own pen and
    the sun, so small, so glorious
rising in a cone of light, sinks
    behind the grey again, leaving
a scar of rosy fire in melting pinks
    and vanishes?

There's no jewel
   we can think of
that's orange. But she
   has studded her hair
with clips and stars
   trailed from her fingers
chains and ropes
   hung from her throat
twin pendants
   in cleavages of water

flung anklets, bracelets
   to bob on circling floats.
She's scattered a fistful
   of uncut gems
over shore and hill, a chip or two
   dropped on a skyline boat;
set five ablaze
   in a row of lamps and saved
for her royal knuckle
   the brightest stone.

But we who pass by railings
   facelessly in twos
past necklaces of traffic
   glass cases banked with jewels
will have to choose
   from local
topaz, tourmaline, citrine
   quartz for there's no
jewel we can think of
   that's orange.

Moons come in all the colours
   of the rainbow. Combine them
too. I wish I could see such moons
   parade themselves night after night
across my window. I wish I could
   keep awake to watch such moons.

And if I could, I'd wish words were
   inks, inks quills for lyres, wish
I could play and sing along with the words
   like Sappho. I'd stand at the window
stripped, take colour from the moon
   as it shone through cloud, marbled me

head to toe, in rainbow. I'd learn
   like Uri Geller, eyes closed, palm
on my belly, moon on my hand, to read
   colour through touch, open my eyes
to have the moon confirm, at a stroke
   the shades we'd been through.

Perhaps I could keep these colours
   under my skin, transmit them
the way you say my eyes change colour
   when we're making love, through
my entire length lying under you
   to your every pore. Then you'd know

know in your bones how to read me
   how to match my moods.
That'd be good. Better than clues
   most men I know are blind to.
Most men are colour-blind did you know?
   when it comes to grey & green & blue.

Why not mention the purple flower
    token of exchange
between this world and the next?
    Ignore the wind

and the wild wet light blossoming
    as the purple does
when you draw the curtain to inspect
    the light but your eye rebounds

from a flower, colour
    you can't quite name.
Purple will do. What does the shade
    under grey stone walls

grey underside of wings you saw
    when the sun blazed
turn blue, cornflower blue as gulls flew
    into the face of the sun

in another lightning exchange, matter?
    Mention the purple, stay close
to the heart: remember
    when the curtain is drawn

on the infinite blue that today
    is infinite grey
it's the heart that knows
    the best in its gift

to exchange for the gift of sky and light
    and though you can't place
its name or shade or hearing
    the cynic's groan at the mere

mention of flowers – oh not again –
    retreat like a snail in your shell
throw shame to the winds, gravitas to the skies
    and do it! – mention the purple.

One sky is a canvas for jets and
    vapour trails, one
Venetian. One a dawn that may spoil
    or bloom, the other
a perfection. On towerblocks or grand
    canals, roundabouts or
basins. Removal trucks, motorbikes
    icecream vans are gilded
in the one, in the other, silence is golden.
    On a moat in Dresden
there are swans, colonnades in water.
    In the Piazetta everyone
is dressed in white, everything is
    lined with copper.

Some will look for immanence
    in a shadow on the wall sinking
through water, or focus where the shadow ends
    on a bricked diagonal of gold
and remember how sun warms brick and linen
    in offices and houses
how glory that was general
    is particular to them.
One is the glory of the yet-to-be, one
    of a past that reminds us
how we've seen it in our own lives exactly
    as it used to be but were
blinded by those lives, distracted from our own
    perfections.

Black fruit is sweet, white is sweeter.
    Sweeter than any white grape, white fig
is white mulberry, too sweet to eat
    without water.

And water, catching casts of berry
    is bluer in its blue-washed pool
than any sky in living memory, boasting
    hot summers in England.

If England is small
    this corner of heaven
is smaller. Barely two bow-lengths
    but morning as long

as the Garden on the Day of Rising
    and evening the length
of a life so little wasted, little room
    has been left for regret.

Instead there is shade and silence.
    One as deep as the other.
Yet for all their depth, buoyant
    as a salt sea, more buoyant for the scent

of jasmine from four corners; only
    tuberose clutches more at the heart
when the heart's at home but home's
    where the heart grows greyer.

So if I were to tell you in future
    how sweet were the berries
left lying in a bowl
    dried and greyed and inedible

once sweet enough to bring tears
    to your eyes, I swear to God
not a word would ring true, for even truth
    lies in the face of the incomparable.

They go right through you, smells.
  Those sweet, back to old childhood
springs, churning your stomach smells.
  Lavender-scented writing paper, violet
Love-Hearts embossed with hearts;
  sweetness grown sickly on tongues
so free with bitterness. Tastebuds develop
  from sweet to sour to bitter but why
should one preclude the other, narcissi
  choking a room with scent, repel?

Let me drink you in, small yellow stars.
  Bury my nose, as children do in donkey's fur
in your blotted skies, your criss-crossed
  shadow lemons. Meet, in the depths
of my lungs, companion smells – bacon
  from boarding-school kitchens, damp from
rotting bridge-struts, juniper's gin and long
  before cowslip, primrose, daffodil –
hyacinth on the *Haft Sin* table. *Sombol
  serkeh, somagh, seeb, seer, sabzeh, samanoo*

seven symbols even Iranians puzzle over.
  They all relate to health, my mother
claims, for example, vinegar is good for
  arthritis, sumac is anti-cholesterol
apples are obvious, garlic, greenery, malt
  all stand for *Salamati*, S for health.
For sweet, salt, sour, an ill-assorted spread
  of comestibles nothing much to look at
but smell them, cook them, taste them . . . Ah!
  Salamat boshid! Blessings for the New Year!

He's tying up the gypsophila
   that lay like a snowspray
on his emerald grass. Dark emerald
   that reminds me of Rilke's
dark evergreen, *our hours of pain.*
   And has flung a bouquet

of dead daisies there. Uprooted
   like aftersmells of love they remind me
of Valentine's smell, *corn and milk*
   coming through her tears.
Are those deadheads still on the pavement
   in that backstreet I think

is Tehran? The walled tree's
   whose mock-stars fall
out of its skirts to a shade
   the width of a smell: a white cocoon
I can enter, stoop in, bow my head
   to a guttering star, bridal-veiled.

And had we ever lived
　in my country
you might have asked
　had I returned

were backstreets cool
　in siesta heat
did hawkers call
　the mulberry thrive

on neglect?
　Who can I ask
of mulberry and mint
　courtyard shade

so alive with presence
　when no one's around
but a burning sun
　and grapes, walled-in?

Who can I ask
　to ensure a return
have me to stay, receive
　my gifts?

Winter's strains
   have surfaced to skin
under bra-strap, thigh elastic
   stone under skull and towel.

As wind blows, sun burns
   I turn to the ground's pull
record in every crease, every
   three-ringed knuckle

the ferocity of white.
   Tonight, against your knees
two shields of red when I
   near you, flashing moon-teeth

to your laughter, blackberry
   nipples to your lips
the nightsky we see by will see us
   by our eyes and teeth, like lamps

cut out on its own black skin
   sickle moons on winter
nights when we, worm-pale, sleep
   in rooms as black as ink.

And in the sea's blackness sank
    wreckage of the day
its faces, voices, stops and starts
    while to the surface rose
lights, lapping of waves
    squawks of invisible birds
we heard as apertures
    in a low dark sky –
the glittering crust that to an eye
    seeing for the first time
evidence of man's night on earth
    might be as intricate, luminous
as space to ours and wondrous
    in its buoyancy, littoral
between depths and heights, electric
    on its charts of glass
as peace might be
    putting out without sound or sail.

When space is at its emptiest
    an undervoice in which
songs of the sea, lamp, grass
    inside one's orbit sing

then space assumes a radiance
    an open throat through which
songs of the sea, lamp, grass
    sing not of themselves but of

something old, something new
    something borrowed, something blue
something, whoever it belongs to
    in which other lives begin.

Was it morning, night?
    I remember
only because I have it
    now – stamped when a baby
was born in those days –
    her footprint.

Blue-inked, small enough
    to fit a notepad
like the first
    inkling of a poem.
What time was it?
    I remember

winter light on that
    boulevard, some park
the Shah had planted
    opposite, how poor it looked
how poor the strollers
    were in their shabby coats

mountain light and rows
    of saplings.
If she asks again
    her time of birth, I'll give her
mountain light and her own
    loveliness, I'll even

give her the name
    of a boulevard, hospital . . .
Apadana . . . Pars . . . everything
    but the amnesia
before
    that footprint.

Curling her tail
   and staring
not quite sure who
   I was
how many kittens
   I too
had had, stalking
   past as
disdainfully
   as blackness
smallness
   warrants, this
is what she
   left me with:
curvature
   and silence.

His 18th. He likes Chinese.
    Café Rouge'll do. I've spent
a fortune on his lamp, lamp to light
    his future, throw light on him.

I see it on a piano, YAMAHA in gold
    torso in shadow, right hand
with his father's fingers – no his own
    plying up and down up and down

though only over a small stretch
    the way it used to drive me mad
make me tear my hair, get rid of him.
    A lamp to light him. Something

to keep forever we both agreed.
    The way my mother's mother
scarved and sunglassed in the sky
    would want it. No pyrotechnics.

While the fireworks in his body
    are what he himself once called
in between the keys. When I first read that –
    of a restaurant he'd have for jazz

he wrote, called *In Between The Keys* –
    something flashed inside me. Like
scattered light, his mother's skirts
    inside him. I dream of him

four years old, abandoned in a bath
    the tears on him. Squib, damp squib.
I taste the salt, his lashes' salt.
    My fingerling. My waterlips.

Staring up from his pram to the sky
    through mobile leaves that so
transfixed him, no matter who smiled
    and cooed, whose head might suddenly
block his light, those sea-washed eyes
    that had never yet seen sea
wouldn't flinch, barely blinked
    and when at last they panned from
tree to you, it would seem as if
    time itself had been scanned
so slowly did sight catch up with vision
    vision give way to a human hold.

And though he'd sit for hours, tearless
    and wide awake, you'd lift him
shoulder him with kisses, words, any
    bauble waved like a flag to bring it
home to him, him home to you.
    But even his eyelashes, so long
and straight, channelled his gaze
    outwards and onwards and irises
so light, so green, implied nothing
    but light behind them, as if his mind
had fled to the back of his skull
    and bled every shadowy lobe.

As you carried him in to a sunless
    hall, behind your back, were
those eyes trained down on a lane
    where the pram still stood?
A white sheet rumpled, an awning
    of leaves shadowed on sheet
and hood. As you shifted his weight
    and revolved to the door
between him and the light, did something
    pass – like a tryst, deferred
drawn up through those eyes to a sky
    he was saying goodbye to?

New Year's Eve.
   Under a sky as high as this
we are cut-glass, space-lattices
   for broken narratives, like
mountain cities left behind
   through the mind's eye, revisited.

Pavement weeds are faint with light.
   Birds raucous in the bushes.
Perspectives in the High Street
   lowered, lengthened, acquire
the clarity of paintings. Glass
   animals of childhood, horses

seals balancing on crystal globes
   are as we are to the sky
whose distance finds no measure
   between cloud and cloud, this year
and the next, being the same high blue
   we saw when we were small

and our menagerie of bright revolves
   already broken narratives.
Against the unbroken blue, nothing
   is not nervous, alive with light:
stream, swans, bicycles, elude our need
   to follow one train of thought

of wing or water, adjacent roofs
   throwing down a flock of birds
like a gauntlet to the wind, stand
   impassive as it lifts, whirls
on a clap of laughter . . . and as we
   on foot, happy to be human, move on.

In this
    country
the brilliance of
    sun on snow
is as though
    not love
but belief in love
    laid its hand on you

you the adolescent
    whose world was always
gilded, warmed
    even on its highest
snows
    and now
every berried branch
    you look up and through

slopes
    of builders' sand
remind you of last year
    when it laid its
hand on you
    gentle
as the turning of a
    calendar.

Here's dusk to burrow in;
    doorstep light where children
going home from school, mothers
    at the open doors of cars
forms having lost their shadows
    when the sun went down

become them. Trailing to peer
    dim-sightedly at a glove on a spike
creature or leaf curled on stone
    coin or charm in the rubble
as if, too late, they were looking
    to learn a landscape they know

wind will shift, night remove
    they freeze, sniff air –
freedom just yards from the warren.
    But thresholds braved today
as tomorrow's beckon, will darken.
    So catch, in the last of the light

the last child, mitten and scarf
    ankle and calf from kerb to car
the snowberry-white last gesture
    for that tail-end of our darkening
forms – *entre chien et loup* – that
    mark and its marked erasure

is the theft and gift, fang and fur
    of dusk, this double vision:
a sighting of metamorphic laws only
    dusk affords with menace and grace
but eyes inscribe, mistakenly
    as last transitions.

All yellow has gone from the day.
    I'm left with the blues and greys.

Pool of light on the desk.
    Strangely content. Perhaps

night is more my element.
    How white white flowers seem

skin showered, oiled, and the day
    but a night away. The days ahead . . .

While the tulip threatens
    to lose one leaf
and a pigeon
    perched on a tile-red roof

grooms another, ruff
    to the light
articulating
    irridescence on its purple patch;

while a small girl plays
    with her football in a coat
as red as tulips
    and my son now smiles at children

being a man;
    as days pass, post comes and goes
without news, across
    empty lots, back gardens

as far as
    waterways to mill towns
these urban tracts between us
    spread

as if they
    could be our river now
and these desks where we ply
    a trade, riverbanks.

Even if I never said
    or said too often what was
on my mind and you wore
    new shoes in plum-bloom

purple I'd made you buy;
    even if you did
head north when we were both
    due south, *if only* was

our only melody line
    and for good or ill, any *even if*
says it's a waste of time, I'd still
    regret and regretting, lie.

Darling, your message on the phone
    made me cry. I phoned you back
to let you hear the tears
    in my voice but your phone
was engaged. On second thoughts
    I'll write you this with
tears gone from my eyes and cloud
    like smoke from smokestacks
moving across a lining of blue
    that is our sky, that no matter
how clouds cross, yes, my smoke rises
    – I'm not smoking now –
we've always known lies behind them
    as the heart and breath behind
your vowels – such a long ah
    in darling! – as tears behind these
words, not sad tears nor tears
    to lay on you, but dried tears to
'open the eyes of the heart'
    as they say back home – and this is
back home – to beginnings we always
    dreamed of, now lay a claim to
not knowing if dreams come true.
    I'd thank you but *'it hasn't a thankyou'*
and I haven't words large and clean
    enough – the phone's ringing now . . .
it wasn't you . . . and this sentence
    if I go on like this is never
going to end as you aren't with me
    nor I with you. I wish I could slice
that bit of the tape and keep it forever
    but neither you nor I know how to.

Is it before or after the fiesta?
   Have the revellers gone in
that the sunflower leans
   like a bystander in shade;
with the bowl of the fountain
   empty, holding last night's
laughter, is the wedding, fiesta
   today? Who are the bride
and groom, sea and sun, heat
   and flesh, in a sprinkler's
arc, are the bridesmaids sparrows
   seen through spray? Why
does an air of expectation meet
   before its joy, regret?

On a late summer's day that draws
    to a close as summer does
– one closing within another –
    I remember tree peonies

deep in shade, globe within globe
    wearing colours on their sleeves
like doublets slashed with crimson
    and regretting how flowers

so gorgeous, luxurious, seemed
    destined to a half-life, even
in their prime only ever
    half-open. Not my kind of flower

I'd half a mind to say.
    Now summer rises, rises
then droops its head. The stem
    of the sky's too weak for sun

lolling its face in shade.
    Summer's a slipped umbrella
the melancholy
    when everything's been said.

First you invite me to tea under your appletree and now
    send me a photograph of where we sat, you, still ill
by your herbs in shade and I in a wedge of sun angled
    under apples. Let me not break the chain. Send you
a poem of your photo of the patio of your new home, wish you
    entirely better. The doorway's as narrow in its light
as shadow's broad and black in the kitchen. Blackest of all
    your bike in silhouette. And the appletree just visible
where bright light grows on a shrub I'd know, if it weren't
    for those clumps of flowering light you knew I'd like
has no flowers. But what can I write that's not in the eye?
    How something tall and narrow can suggest a yardage of sun
an L, one arm of which you'll plant, where drainpipes ask for disguise
    with shade-lovers? How, in a city's heart, Elephant & Castle
you can be in the heart of the country, how knee-high trellises
    fronting allotments whose tenants stop to talk to you, spell
an other worldliness? But you know all that. How memory
    speaks to the image, image to the word. How inadequate
we are in our borrowings, not knowing if by saying *I'm like you*
    we do violence. Thank you for the herbs, tea, the photo.
Think of this as a postcard but more than that, a short time
    spent in your company, after the event, a recognition of those
differences we run into now and then, alternatives we never chose –
    patios with loaded apple-trees, herb troughs, neighbouring
histories of architects and saints in the churches of south London;
    other people's knowledge vaguely interesting, vaguely boring
lifestyles, lovelives and sometimes even illnesses worn transparent
    on a face that brings it home: the equity no one has in common;
differences that now and then make us feel are of less account
    than an hour or two – and I hate that word affirming but –
affirming, the way women do when we say *me too*, each other.
    (And the facings of your bookshelves like an opening accordion.)

Everywhere you see her, who could have been
    Monet's woman with a parasol
who's no woman at all but an excuse for wind –
    passage of light-and-shade we know
wind by – just as his pond was no pond
    but a globe at his feet turning to show
how the liquid, dry, go topsy-turvy, how far
    sky goes down in water. Like iris, agapanthus
waterplants from margins where, tethered
    by their cloudy roots, clouds grow underwater
and lily-floes, like landing-craft, hover
    waiting for departure, she comes at a slant
to crosswinds, currents, against shoals of sunlight
    set adrift, loans you her reflection.
I saw her the other day I don't know where
    at a tangent to some evening, to a sadness
she never shares. She wavers, like recognition.
    Something of yours goes through her, something
of hers escapes. To hillbrows, meadows
    where green jumps into her skirt, hatbrim shadows
blind her. To coast, wind at her heels, on diagonals
    as the minute hand on the hour, the hour
on the wheel of sunshades. Everywhere you see her.
    On beaches, bramble paths, terraces of Edwardian
hotels. In antique shops, running her thumb along
    napworn velvet. A nail buffer. An owl brooch
with two black eyes of onyx. Eyes she fingers.
    But usually on a slope. Coming your way.

Don't draw back
   his lilac said.
Don't pin me down
   his blue and grey.
Whose tears are pricking
   eyelids? asked his pink
on snow. Mine, black answered
   mine that light can't shed.

Light comes between us and our grief:
    flushes it out with gold.
And when skies are overcast, still
    we collude with clouds, building
grey to a spur for light that will
    drive us to stand at a distance
from ourselves, small at the barricades
    clouds burst to let grief go.
Light leaves us bereft in one sense
    only to flood us with sensation
bleeding out grief in a bright dissolve.
    There's something I can't hold
in the presence of light, great light, or feel
    as a river might feel for its stones.

Why does the aspen tremble
   without a trace of wind?
Under its spire, close
   your eyes, listen.
Listen to Khadijah. Her
   big heart beating.
He is bringing a new wife
   home today. Half her age.
Twice her beauty. Aisha, Aisha.
   Listen to the leaves.
What the Bosnian Moslem women say.
   The story they weave.

Khadijah is not jealous.
   Under the lintel she
stands, arms folded.
   Arms she will open wide.
Large, generous Khadijah
   ample-limbed . . .
A horse pricks up its ears
   backs two paces, whinnies.
And a current, faint
   as the morning star, runs
through her, air around her
   ripples, stills.

Like an arrow shot from
   a quiver, that impulse
loosed from her heart
   is caught in the arms
of aspen, sends a shiver
   through every leaf.
And thereafter, though there are
   no aspens in Arabia
though there is
   no wind, this is why
the aspen trembles
   over the bed's thin stream.

Boys have been throwing
    stones all day; even
the youngest – barely two –
    could throw stones that reached

the water. Years ago
    you threw them too from a beach
or bank and I, whose throws
    even dogs disdain, valiantly tried

to skim them.
    I read in Sylvia's diary
of stones the colour of fox – and so they are
    from a distance.

Apricot stones, filters.
    I bury them under a red-fox coat
of shingle. Camouflage
    so much of the past in my rush

to near the future. Far away as ever.
    Whatever the shore, wherever
the blue, letters locked in drawers
    rowboats, wells

in dogeared snapshots, postcards sent
    but mysteriously
repossessed years later –
    hidden pockets of a globe

we once called home
    are still at home and will
when I least expect, resurface
    in the gap between

boy and girl, whose stones soar
    and sink without trace
or land, marked
    'return to sender'.

Foreshortened
   light claws out of the sea
skin-puckered. Reluctant
   to leave the great outdoors
– benchwood warm –
   huddles behind grey towels.
Light's eyes are blurry with
   salt, heels white with water.

Fists knuckled and locked
   against his mouth, scanning
a roughening shore, he squints, wavers . . .
   Makes to go then, dropping
his towels, shoulder-blades twin
   gleams of sun, he's back in the swim
to brave out the day as
   yours lengthens.

On a diving-board, against
    a centrefold of sky they queued:
eyes rheumy, hair plastered, scars
    whitening under welts of pus
and queue there still as if
    in the after-image, sparkling off
into scythes of light, were the gold
    and ground of every plunging replay.

Knowing replay is not countless
    that water and its breaking
close on a lap behind them
    was it for this that they
showed no mercy, shrieking, shoving
    the weakest from the highest board
clowning about with variants
    on the perfect fall from grace?

Wanting nothing less than a commandment
    for themselves to hurl, shatter, resurface
into their features, for this they held
    nose and breath, plummeting faster
than the speed of sight, fell and kept on
    falling until, in that last recall
higher than the highest board, they froze
    in that blue inhuman air?

These hills are literally blue.
    And ryegrass pink
not with a setting sun but
    in the lie of grain, underside
of plaited heads wind's wave
    combs through.

As night comes close
    this far north, nearly
two months after midsummer's eve
    still light at eleven and
enormous skies nowhere near the end
    of their travelling show, wind

whips at my hair, tugs loose
    my clothes. Wrenches
out of my eyes, ears, frozen pen
    a scene, like the line
a croft, a tree and a Highland moon
    cleared to stand alone.

I have removed the scaffolding
　　from the Parthenon. In the city
of the mind's eye, acropolis of
　　dawn, now scaffold it with rays.

I have turned its north face to face
　　east, ramparts into London smog
and where blue begins its columns rise
　　where blue is clear, they end.

As for height, I have left it where
　　it was, dwarfed in the eyes of Gods
at whose feet my chimney pots are
　　fat, terracotta statuettes.

In place of white Pentelic marble, I summon
　　time as a counterweight. Time
in the guise of sun too high for rays.
　　And imagination too slow to keep pace.

Summon them in the name of lightness
　　for by their own dead weight
they make our images so weightless
　　that even in this short span, despite

millennia stone survives, this
　　atonement, my monument to memory
has gone up in smoke, left nothing
　　but a few clouds to bar its trace.

So high up in a house
   being alone is ethereal
like a wind curled up on its ankles
   precarious in a tree

or lung-stain of a shadow
   in a corner of an attic
you can't inhabit as every breath
   must leave its branch

hoarsely clamber down
   to converse with what is real.
So why delay? Is being alone
   the greater love, the greater loss

the ineffable, unreal: touch
   of a cold cheek rosy
in a lower room too much
   the open sore that never bleeds?

These homes in poems –
    how large they were. Upwards
and sideways. How they housed
    in sun and gloom, those loved
unloving fathers' ghosts
    mothers medicinal as scents
that drifted in from trees
    with unusual names.

These homes had attics, tea-chests.
    Country or cathedral views
woodsmoke like epitaphs
    scrawled indelibly on air.
Air was always resident.
    Charged with the many duties
loss imposes on a habitation
    whose owners are elsewhere.

(Air must don its apron, dust
    shafts of light, shake out
camphor and cobweb, breathe
    rings on the bell.) Above all
there was singing. As if the mind
    had climbed to its highest
landing, from an upstairs room
    someone's voice.

And the house rose only
    that this voice should be
embodied, bulwarked against
    wind by walls, rooted
in nursery furniture, friendships
    only flyleaves know
married to its elements, skeleton
    and soul and carried downstairs.

For those who have no homes like
    these, no fork in the road to mark
their winding route from others'
  ·   let the house that the song sings
into being serve as a stopping-inn
    to share a couch, pass the jug
resing the song that will carry
    over wilderness and mountain.

For you, who are
  a large man, a large
man and a delicate poet, whose
  flagstoned hall I have
stood on the brink of, ice-
  blue walls been warmed in

and learned, looking at your
  wife, your beautiful
wife – and you think so too –
  how warm ice-blue can be
like an aureole for eyes
  of blue, Nordic hair of honey

and slept in white and blue
  on an empty floor
at the top of your house
  padded in socks on carpet
to a bathroom through books
  and books you have lived through

and that living-through I catch
  a glimpse of, too awed
to envy, empties me till I am only
  filled with a sense of books
unread, life unlived, a span
  of time and space out there

much too late for the taking
  but not for lifting
as I did the patchwork quilt
  of blue on white, a corner of . . .
for you, I felt like writing
  a line, out of the blue, a poem.

When
    against a cloth
of blue
    silver linings are
reversed
    then, unfrocked
like a single
    diamond drop
vested head to toe
    in blinding white
light enters
    as *Der Rosenkavalier.*

The gate has
   five bars and five
bars of song
   for whatever reason I might
want to sing
   as I climb the stile to a
solitude
   escaping from itself
in smoke-filled rooms
   would be more than enough
to swing me
   as the river does
white heifer on the hill
   from the
dark side of solitude
   to its light-starved
underside
   silver-fir green.

I'm reading with the light on
      though it's 4 o'clock in the afternoon
and the skylight overhead, masked
      with a calico blind, casts
a whiteness in the air as if a blanket
      of snow had covered the pane
and light was filtering through flakes.
      Outside, the freshness, suspense

of after-rain. So the reading-lamp
      behind my shoulder, casting
a small gold glow, is relegated
      by natural light to illumination
that only alters colour. But since
      I'm reading poetry, that small gold glow
having little to do with visibility and
      from a source outside my vision, seems

to have taken upon itself the task
      of a farmstead light at the end of a path
when you first emerge from a forest –
      light that the poem heads towards
or has come from, light you don't read
      lines by but between them by, warming
as the page descends. And when the page
      is turned, the glow recedes so that

lamplight, skylight, gold and snow
      merge and the first words you read
The dandelion does not yet blossom here
      pull you back to their own
gold, light, snow, sky, up on to a ridge
      – the old road between farmsteads? –
leaving the poem out in the open
      and the forest on the page.

Times are – thinking about new wine
    in old bottles – when the mind
flooded with sensations only
    the old words make sense of, tastes
as if never before, their delicacy
    of invention, proof of the pudding.
Such a dawn was this: of promise
    and illusion, birds' proverbial choruses.

I mourn the untold usages still
    redolent of grape, of yeast, if I had
new eyes, ears for the daily round
    they sprang from, mediations
between man, nature, beast, little altered
    in a world as young as ours – evil
being no disease of age, corruption
    no condition of maturing.

I mourn their number
    and their ease. Reading
won't bring them back. Rather
    drive them further back to the cask
the cave they were laid down in –
    the mouth and mind that framed them
mouth and mind that now
    consign them to the bin.

Unless, that is, we read the world
    that informed them with the same
immediacy we assume when we read
    or word our own, and by doing so
find how the same words fit.
    John, at dawn today I read your book
– as I wrote you, and I'll write it twice –
    caught between two sleeps.

Like old red gold welded
    by rhythm where the words
have cracked
    snatches of a poem
set behind my back, keep setting
    as the sun does.

I recite them
    not by memory, by heart.
The rooms of memory
    are dark. Rooms of the heart
flared with dreams where
    blur-faced as white pansies

children lining windows
    thumb their nose
at memory, go
    fishing about in the bloodstream
for slips of the tongue
    figures of speech, puns

that work both day and night.
    Work
and then run out.
    What heart knows is rumbled
molten, eroded, with nothing to cling to
    but love. Memory's

a bad mother, neither oral
    nor literate.
Heart has her number
    holds her to
her smell, bare bones
    the heart's refrain like rock.

An Iranian professor I know asked me
   the first time we met, as he'd asked so many
students: *Saheb-del* – how would you say in English
   saheb-del, can you translate it? And each time
he pronounced the words his fingers tolled the air
   like a bell, a benediction. Years have passed.

Saheb means master, owner, companion; *del*
   means heart. Heart's companion, keeper?
Heart's host? And in those years I've asked
   friends who in turn have asked friends
who know Urdu, Farsi, and no one has come up with
   the English for *Saheb-del*. Is it a name

for the very thing that won't translate? And why
   don't I remember having heard it said?
They say it of people who are hospitable, 'godly'
   I'd say it of the professor himself. Trust him
to keep asking, us to keep failing, and if we can't recall
   its tone, tenor, with what word shall we keep faith?

I've always grown
   in other people's shade.
Not for shelter
   in solidity, neither they
being spreading oak or beech nor I
   some shrinking violet

but when a face upturned
   towards frail light, a voice
that interweaves between
   dark leaves a space for
flower, path for thorn, catch something
   of light's reach and axiom

then lower on the stem
   my edges breathe, droop
through dust re-invents desire
   not for gloss but growth
from this common soil, that upward
   thrust from lateral roots

to a realm
   wholly natural, and radical.
When a face, a voice
   like new leaves on a vane
promise turn by turn
   a view, on a spiralling belt

towards that light, then
   being roused I know
while upholding the crown
   in whose shade I too
throw shadow, I draw
   a freight of light in tow.

. . . Human beings must be
taught to love
silence and darkness.

But in silence comes
    the seepage of
a gas fire's breath

in darkness the pink
    of a child's
mosquito net – it seems

their very presence
    is that love
for how else can we invoke

afterworlds without
    voice, light
but through things that

breathe and move, obey
    an absence
that is deified because

absence is unbearable
    unless, in a residue
of breath and light

we bear the agony
    of presence, and do
call this bearing, loving?

Nothing can ruin the evening –
    car doors slammed, voices raised
in the last of the light, voices
    without owners. And that's
a difference between art and nature –
    art transforming – voices, traffic
tawdriness – but in a gathering-in
    an almost selfish motion; nature
extending outwards as the shore its arms
    night its stars, an open invitation.

The palace of a ship at night
    blinking stars like cursors;
those disembodied voices from
    who knows which shore, drunk –
why note them, fail them?
    Torn between life and art, why is one
without the other like a shore without its sea
    night without its stars, why am I
– still beautiful – so unable to contain
    the ugliness, my own, in either?

It's the eye of longing
        that I tire of
the eye of fantasy
        lost in the grey horizons.

Having neither the heart
        nor talent for
invention, why should I
        – no child of mist –

be party to this cold
        imagination, its cloak
and hood, smuggled goods
        its faery in the dingle?

Where are my sunlight's
        givens? Near the sun
and far from folk
        an albino child, skin clean

as silver, hair white as
        snow, under the Simorgh's
eye as she flies
        over the Alborz Mountains

years later will hear her cry:
        . . . behold my might,
For I have cherished thee beneath my plumes
And brought thee up among my little ones

before she ferries him home
        gives him a feather to light
as a signal
        in times of trouble.

But this is my borrowed plumage
        language, more strange to me
than this foster-tongue, this English
        fairy godmother.

To be so dependent on sunlight
   – small desires on the lookout
gull feathers snagged on slates –
   is to be, in a climate
doomed to cloud, its changing mind
   a paler version of the story:
he whose glory flew away from him
   three times in the shape of a bird
whose wingspan was so great that rain
   could never fall but when faith
at last deserted him and falsehood
   took its place, fall it did to prove
that glory goes back to God, resides
   with God, by any other name.

What is he looking for
   the great white sun
throwing the force of his search
   like torchlight onto the sea?
What he looks for
   will be present
only as long as his looking:
   what he fails to find
absent
   to the precise extent
of his brightness
   blinding himself by reflection
while the passerby takes in
   a high sun, a broken

and a peninsula of violet
   the translation between.
It's darkness
   the white sun looks for
the one thing
   by the light of his eyes
he'll never see; one thing
   the brighter, further
he throws his rays
   the more recedes: it's
his shadow that he looks for
   and will never know
if it is God or self, friend or foe
   if it follows or precedes.

It lives in crystal, flame.
   At night like any man
creeps into a cave; moves
   by stealth, coming and going
by starlight, carrying tatters
   in its mouth, nimbus in its hair.

Who can tell on water
   if shadow's nibbling into light
or light at shadow's edge? Thus
   it is mouth and tail, tail
and mouth, ice or thaw, none knows
   which way they face.

It scavenges on breath.
   It is ear and voice, voice
and ear, by these it mates.
   Eradicates, illuminates
hunches down to ponder
   how weak, how bright, its chain.

As wave comes in on wave
    so light on light
but the one being
    visible, divisible
the other a metamorphosis
    by stealth

serves only to remind one
    how the mountain of
a life, growing to its star
    station, moon station
sun station and finally
    to the utmost limit of the sky

has all the while
    been burning, there
where poppies rout
    the dust, a fire to keep
blood moving, on the foothills
    of an outlawed faith.

It is said
    God created a peacock of light
and placed him
    in front of a mirror.
In the presence
    of God, being so ashamed at his own
beauty, his own
    unutterable perfection, the peacock

broke out in a sweat.
    From the sweat of his nose, God created
the Angels.
    From the sweat of his face, the Throne, Footstool
Tablet of Forms, the Pen
    the heavens and what is in them.
From breast and back
    the Visited House, prophets, holy sites, etc.

From the sweat of his two feet
    God created, from east to west, the earth.
The sea is
    glistening peacock sweat.
Tarmac too.
    From sweat of the peacock's feet of pearl
comes my window view.
    Perhaps I am formed from a trembling

drop on his ankle.
    Cypress, sunflower, bicycle wheels
grass dried in heat
    to the colour of wheat, all, all are
peacock water, peacock dew
    shame and beauty, salt and light
God's peacock
    in his consciousness, walks over.

Too much light is tiresome.
  Knowing this, today's
keeps its counsel. Tight-lipped
  the sky has closed its door
against the sea which
  like an aimless child
spreadeagles on its bed. The day
  is set aside for function.

Every shrub, roof, windowsill
  broods on its own
injunctions. Even birds on errands
  forget to play on thermals
winging it straight across the sky
  as though time and light
were the same thing, same task
  and every bird and bush accountable.

Light's sharpening
  knives of water.
I long for the coolness
  of a room downstairs.
White grapes. A morning
  cigarette. To take
umbrage behind hessian
  blow on a glass
of tea, sugarlump held
  between my teeth, taste
how bitterness
  too quickly sweetens.

Light's packed its water
  of knives in drawer
upon drawer of
  darkness. Where sea's
banded in shadow. Laid
  smaller silvers
out in the calm: glimmer
  of tines, crests
salvers and scoops, flatware
  embossed on handles.
And that downstairs room
  never to have, never to hold

the way Proust says
  on meeting with colons
that inviolate pause
  when a gathering falls silent
before it intones
  has brought him, while
reading, the scent of a rose
  which has never evaporated
though centuries' old, there it comes
  with its teas and spoons
luminous fridge, against the light
  bowed silhouettes of people.

I've stored all the light
    I need. Stored it
in the dark jars of my body.
    Light's in its phase
of falling. Souring, sweetening.
    Boring us with its constancy

polishing, straightening. Light's
    like a grandmother tiring
pushing a strand of hair behind
    her ear, knees aching, sighing.
No one looks up, the sky's too bright.
    Four boys on seaweed ledges.

We look at the sea instead or
    inward to reservoirs
four-handled jars, fats and oils
    seven-herb pickle, smoked fish, spice
down to the cold slabs of our stores
    under bone and cartilage.

I loved you so much
   I couldn't bear the thought
of cold water on you
   dripping from your chin, hands

running down your elbow
   as you lifted your face to the sound
of footsteps. Smiled at me
   through water. Even

when the season turned
   and no one walked out of shade
to burn in sun
   you'd run the cold –

how cold your hands were.
   Nowhere, as the season turns
and I walk from shade
   or the smell of shade on a sunless

street, in and out of the shade
   of trees to find
no difference, will someone again
   bowing a silvery

head to a tap, move me
   to the kind of love that registers
on skin's temperature
   every shade of difference.

Air's utterly soft, back to its habitual
    cardigans and greys. Relief or regret?
I think of Jane, how she must have felt
    once her house was stripped of visitors.
Of myself. In days when they came en route
    to the States, Iran, bringing
their lifestyles with them. How they left.
    Leaving the house like a house

shorn of heatwave. Where a suitcase
    had been, how amplified the space.
Turmeric stains, a pot misplaced
    how aftershave can linger. And voices
of our own lives, resentful, neglected
    beginning to call from far away.
Or in another language – theirs. Crossing
    each other's waves upstairs, downstairs

making the town seem bigger, smaller
    its centre somewhere to go to
every day. Jane and all the immigrants
    whose families come to visit, overstay
their welcome, leave us holding our life
    in two cupped hands, bewildered at
its lightness, like a fledgeling's, wondering
    why it is they who have flown the nest.

And suppose I left behind
   a portrait inadvertently
like a showercap on a peg
   of this seaview that is hers
and insinuated between its clouds
   strange glimpses of myself
that would alter her view
   not only of me but of the sky
her mornings open out on or
   worse, something of herself

either way some hurt would unfold
   open out its own cloud, like smoke
would streak her air. Her air of . . .
   Seeing ourselves beautiful
also hurts. No longer what we are
   what we were we love but cannot claim.
Looking up, each time we do
   is a silver seachange pencilling
light, shading, erasing
   each time, each time a change.

And where is the singular moment
   unwritten, that's free of pain?
As if by magic, silver lines
   of the horizon have disappeared.
A black ship rides on grey.
   Between everything is a distance
by which we know ourselves, ever
   smarting in the gaps, between
clouds, ships, a child and his unseen
   parents walking on ahead.

'Going away'
　　is not so much
a going away as a
　　coming towards that

part of ourselves which
　　in our daily lives
seems so curiously
　　absent, distant, then here

away from home, in a snatch
　　of song from a beach
at dusk, so endearingly, so
　　agonizingly close.

Finally, in a cove
    that cups thin fog
like a hand its thirst
    this indivisibility of
sea and sky like a grey
    pearl between two claws

makes sense: as if a bay
    waisting a horizon, woman
legs twined around a man
    were what were needed
to make the horizontal
    more beautiful, more felt;

to interpose
    between eye and sense
a possibility in containment
    of the infinite becoming part
of what the eye can never see
    but the sense can comprehend.

*

It can come from the simplest
   of things: a room
tidied, new folders slipped
   from cellophane;
how a ballpoint runs
   without smudging or
looking up through smoke
   blue spiral veils
how your eyelashes
   become nets for light
so wherever you look
   light can't escape.

What makes it shimmer?
   The irrational and static
glow that invades and
   expands a space till
like a bubble full to bursting
   poised, infrangible
skin meets the outmost
   reaches of its waves.
And the shimmering starts.
   Thickens. Radiance
solidifies to a volume
   you can walk in, wear.

Dangerous, being so sheer
   it's also safe.
You wear it like a mantle, aura
   a superstition
you must not name.
   You call it *the shining*
secretly to yourself.
   Follow it down the street
carry upstairs to unwrap
   so its perfume fills the room
like flowers waiting for water . . .
   Make it wait.

Inside its capsule, time's
    both a sentence you
must run with, grappling
    blind corners, pursuing
a flare, and a silence
    coiled, sprung to mime
every flicker and feint
    in an eye, an ear . . .
don't lag behind, don't rush it.
    All you have to go on
is how footfalls sound, shining
    dims, trust and prayer.

Who put it there? You did.
    Who can again at will?
You can. What are its talismans?
    Desire, despair. See
how it came this morning
    from loneliness, boredom
a hint of rain; a move to
    call it in as you might a boat
rise to it as if to dawn
    tell someone else what you
call it. Dare it to live up to
    rise above, such names.

What is the light we walk into
    bathe in, wake to?
Of the two lights that it is –
    one sky's, the hour's
orientation of a room
    riveting in slants, slow
pirouettes, the other –
    what is that though?
that comes to meet the first.
    As if our daily darknesses
half-felt had, sooner or later
    to see the light of day.

Our own light I mean.
   Some sleeping thing
that rises, like a fawn
   from bracken, half-dazed
at its own liquidity . . .
   what fusion is it made for?
Flesh with its source of being
   silhouette and sun
in the open hand of a clearing
   or occluded green
the heart's dissolve, to die in
   be stripped of flame?

What deaths of ego, cynicism
   cowardice must we undergo
clinging to those darknesses
   we feed like ravenous mouths
forego, to unveil the simple
   moment, that open hand
on ours, both fingering back
   the curtain to reveal
a single ray? Of truth maybe
   aligning its core between
two lights, their shining eclipsed
   as its own is newly named.

Notes and Dedications